Thame
in old picture postcards

by Norman Waters

European Library ZALTBOMMEL/THE NETHERLANDS

INTRODUCTION

Thame is a market town situated about three miles north of the M40, and is forty-five miles from London and thirteen miles from Oxford. It is a town of some antiquity, sited upon a sloping ridge above the flood plains of the river Thame, and was first settled in Celtic times. Its name comes from the Celtic 'Tam' meaning quiet and still, the Saxons called it Tama. There are no traces of it being a Roman settlement, and its first mention in history was in 675. Urns from this period were found in the area in 1858. It was around the fifth and sixth centuries that the town began to gain any importance. In 921, an army of Danes encamped in the town and erected fortifications. That the town was by now an important one, was shown by it being granted the dignities of a burg, by a charter by Wulfere, King of Mercia. In the year 971, the Archbishop of York, Archbishop Oskytel, died in the town, showing that Thame must have reached sufficient status for such a personage to visit by this time.

The market charter was granted in 1215, by King John to Bishop Hugh Trotman, and confirmed by Henry III. It was because of the market that the upper High Street is 190 feet wide, being one of the widest streets of Medieaval construction in the country. This divides the town, with Buttermarket on the cool north, being a narrow street, then Middle Row with the broad expanse of Cornmarket on the south side. Bishop Henry Lexington increased the revenue of the market, by diverting the Aylesbury-Oxford road to run through the town centre. The cattle market is no longer held in the High Street, as is the Tuesday market, as a special site was provided for this off North Street in 1951.

The present town hall, which was erected in 1887 to commemorate Queen Victoria's jubilee, stands on the site of an earlier Elizabethan market hall, and possibly the original site of the market cross. On the third Thursday in September, Thame Agricultural Show is held on the show site along the Kingsey road about half a mile outside the town. This is of considerable size, attracting entries from all over the country, and may become a two-day event in the near future. It started as a ploughing match between two ploughmen, this leading to an annual event which started on the 25th of October 1855, and it has been held every year since then, apart from the war years. A fair is held in the town, which lasts three days, and occupies the whole of the centre of the town from Bell Lane to the War Memorial. Another fair which is a charter fair, at which horses were sold, and servants were hired, is still held for two days during the second week in October, and occupies only the Upper High Street as far as the War Memorial.

The town possesses a wealth of well-preserved old buildings, and presents a. pleasant uneven skyline to the eye, as no two buildings are of the same height. It is for these reasons the Council for preservation of rural England has listed it as one of fifty-two towns considered to be worthy of preservation. The Church of Saint Mary's, the parish church, is a splendid building, particularly for a town of this size. Its building was commenced in 1240, by Bishop Grosseteste, on the site of an earlier church. It is built of local stone, and due to alterations and extensions, work continued through the reign of Henry VIII, the last alteration being in 1673 when the last perpendicular window was inserted in the west of the church. It is pure cruciform in design, being 151 feet in length and 96 feet in breadth. The finest thing in its interior is a fourteenth century screen, which is a stone design executed in wood. During the Civil War it was used as barracks, a prison, stables and as a hospital. The north wall still bears the scars made by bullets when the Roundheads laid seige to the building during their advance upon the town.

Close by the church is the Prebendal, obscured from direct view by its charming gatehouse. The chapel was built about 1241, and until the erection of Saint Joseph's Church, was used as the Roman Catholic place of worship. The most famous of the prebendaries was Cardinal Henry Beaufort, who became Bishop of Winchester and Lord Chancellor of England. All that remains of the old building is the chapel and the monks' dormitory. It is now a private residence. In Church Road will be found the Tithe barn, which has fine examples of 'brick nogging', within its timber frame. Also there is the Old Boy's Grammar School, founded by an endowment of Lord Williams, who was a member of the court of Queen Elizabeth I. Building was commenced in 1569, and it first opened as a school in 1570. In the grounds, alongside the road, are the Almshouses, which represent a fine example of Elizabethan architecture. The town is well known for the fact that John Hampden died in the building that was then the Greyhound Inn, from wounds received at the battle of Chalgrove during the Civil War. A native born of the town, however, who is worthy of note is John Holt, who rose to be England's Lord Chief Justice. He was educated at the Grammar School in Thame and proved to be a man of great integrity. Another well known local figure was James Figg who was reputed to be the best boxer in the country.

The town offers an interesting selection of inns, all of them old, most of them unspoilt by modernisation, both inside and out. The most fascinating of these is the Bird Cage, built in the early fifteenth century. The upper floors were once used to house lepers and its cellars to house Napoleonic prisoners of war, and is reputed to be haunted. It was here that the local Masonic Society was formed. Fortunately, the town has not been spoilt by modern development, as this has been confined to the outskirts of the town.

Since the end of the 1940's, the towns population has increased greatly, accommodated by the erection of several small, well-sited housing developments, and one very large one to the east. There is no longer a railway service in the area. Beyond the railway station is the Industrial Estate, and a large petroleum depot. Lord Williams' school is now in a large modern building to the west of the town, with the new Sports and Arts Centre in its grounds. Apart from the fact that the Upper High Street has been paved for use as a car park, with trees planted there, Thame can be seen today looking practically the same as it has for hundreds of years.

My grateful thanks to Mrs. Bishop, Mrs. Cleaver, Joan Davies, Mrs. Fleet, Doug Mott, Willox G. MacKenzie, Michael Newitt, Avis Penn, Bill Reading and 'Smudge' for the kind loan of their old photographs. In conclusion, my particular thanks to Doctor Andrew Markus and Maureen Poulter for their encouragement to produce this book, also to my wife Patricia and daughter Diane for their help in its preparation.

1. Before market halls were built, the market site was marked by a cross, which symbolised the protection and blessing of the church over all who attended there. The first market hall in Thame was erected in Elizabethan times and probably stood on the site of the cross. The hall in this photograph was built by the Earl of Abingdon in 1684, originally standing on pillars to allow market trading to be carried on beneath it, later these being filled in. It was used as a courtroom, trials usually being held monthly, and also to house the offices of the town council. The odd looking protrusion to the left of it housed a spiral staircase.

Girls' Grammar School, Thame.

2. The Girls' Grammar School, seen here at about 1890, was erected as a town mansion house, by the Knolleys family in 1572, and was one of the finest buildings in the town. In 1840 it became the Oxford County School for Boys, then from 1908 the Girls' Grammar School, by which name it was known until it was demolished. This school was founded by Miss Todd in 1841 at 40 Upper High Street, moving to this much larger building in 1908. Its final use was for the storage and distribution of electronic components, today the site is occupied by Tesco and Co-operative supermarkets.

GIRLS GRAMMAR SCHOOL
THAME OXON. Nº 4

3. During the French Revolution, the building was occupied by French refugees, believed to be priests. They were little more than prisoners, being restricted in their movements and not allowed to leave the town. The arch to the right of the building was one of the finest examples of an Elizabethan arch in the country. As a school, it had a covered swimming pool, a gymnasium, with buildings and gardens reaching back to Southern Road. The area so occupied was known as Burgage plots, and were behind all the premises on the south side of the High Street. The origins of these are obscure, but it is believed that they were provided for the shopowners to grow produce, or keep livestock on. In the fourteenth century there were 76 of them, let at a rent of one shilling per year.

Highstr. Thame.

4. From the junction of the Lower High Street and Bell Lane, the High Street widens. In the centre being the Town Hall, and behind it, Middle Row. This scene is very much the same today, as most of the buildings are conserved and relatively unspoilt. The exceptions are behind the horse and cart on the right of the photograph, where Walkers' Seedsmen and Nurserymens Shop, and the old Girls' Grammar School have been demolished and replaced with modern buildings. Also to the left of the High Street, one large old shop, Rouse's, has been demolished and replaced with smaller shops.

5. The Misses Walker, outside their sixteenth century sweet and tobacco shop at 1 Cornmarket, in the 1880's. This has been used as a tobacconists for over one hundred years, and is still trading as such today. The tall chimney to the left of the photograph, is that of the boiler for the Public Baths. The sign advertising these can still be seen painted on the wall in Buttermarket. It reads 'Thame Bath House. Public Baths 6d. Tuesdays, Fridays and Saturdays'.

TOWN HALL, THAME, OXON
H. M

6. Thame Town Hall and High Street, taken about 1900. The building above the girl's head was then the Anchor Inn, now an estate agents, but like all the buildings in the photograph, still looking the same today, apart from the change of use of the shops, this side of the High Street is unspoilt. The area in front of the Town Hall is now used as a car park. The second building from the left, was formerly the Greyhound Inn, where John Hampden died. The area of the street just out of the photograph to the right, is the only part of the town where buildings have been demolished.

7. The Six Bells public house, in about 1890, it is situated in the Lower High Street. Its sign now bears the legend, on one side 'The last Inn out', on the other 'The first Inn in'. This was not always so, as the house at Priestend corner now known as 'The Old Crown' was the furthest from the town centre towards Oxford. The front of the Six Bells is very different today. The cottage to the left is now part of the inn, and it has a frontage of mock Tudor appearance. The row of cottages to the left is still there, although they now have been restored and look rather better today.

8. Thame Lower High Street, from the bottom end of the High Street, in late Victorian times. Today there is a restaurant, outside of which the ladies would have been standing, and the large tree is no longer there. The three-storied building by the lamp post is from the Victorian era, next to this stands a cruke built building, a grocers, at this time 'Mussons'. The owner of this business used to deliver the groceries in a pony and trap to the outlying farms in the area.

9. Thame fair, about 1907, during the September Show Fair. Standing out clearly in the centre of the roundabout, is the very ornate steam-driven organ. This site, in front of the Town Hall, is today the traditional site for the Galloping Horses roundabout, during Thame Show Fair. The style of clothing worn by the people in the picture, is an excellent record of the fashions of this period. Also worthy of note is the ornate baby carriage. The fair caused considerable chaos in the town, as until recent years, the showmen parked their caravan homes on the footpaths, leaving only a few feet between them and the shops and buildings.

10. Looking from the bottom of Grammar School Hill (formerly Christmas Hill), across the Ford Bridge on the Oxford Road. Where the figure stands is Priestend. The building behind him being the cottage from where the Roundhead troops were first seen advancing on Thame during the Civil War. It was formerly a shepherd's cottage, and a carving of a sheep can still be seen on the roof today. The barn on the left has long since disappeared, and a garage occupies this position today. The open drains, running in front of the walls can be seen here, with the bridges over them giving access to the properties on the right.

11. The ford in 1908, a period in which the roads were considerably improved, the bridge having been built to bypass the ford. The row of cottages behind the signpost has been demolished, and their site has become part of Rycotewood Agricultural College, which occupies the buildings that were formerly the workhouse. Of a sight seen at the ford in 1871, a medical inspector, Doctor Buckeman, wrote, after commenting on the foul contents of various open gutters and ditches, flowing into the river above the ford *...and in the centre of the ford downstream, stood a barrelcart, into which the driver was ladelling the contents of the river, the destination of which was a certain local brewery where it was to be converted into beer.*

THAME, OXON. WITH THE HOUSE WHERE JOHN HAMPDEN DIED.   TAUNT & CO. 10

12. The north side of the High Street in the early 1900 period, with the Town Hall to the right. The buildings to the left continue on through Buttermarket. Most of the shop owners displayed their wares on the broad pavements, as can be seen here. The two shops, the one with the wheelbarrow outside, the other being number 106, are in the premises which was the Greyhound Inn. The shop with the tall chimney was the Public Bath House. This is one of the few places in the town where the roofs of the buildings are nearly level.

S G Payne & Sons, Aylesbury. 510.   *High Street*   *Thame*

13. High Street, north side, from Cornmarket about 1903. The building to the extreme right today has a large enamel plate, sited near the first-floor window, bearing the legend '6d Bazaar'. This was uncovered during restoration work, the premises now being a jewellers shop. The interest of both adults and children in the photographer is apparent in this picture, and also the great variety of goods on display outside the shops. Some of the awnings were fastened to metal posts, that were permanently fixed into the pavements.

14. Taken in 1876, a great deal of change can be seen in this and later photographs, as several buildings have been demolished and newer ones built in their place. This view is of the north side of Corn-market, which makes up the south side of Middle Row. The building to the right was Putman's Chandlers, who supplied rick covers etc., and later became Barclays Bank. The horse and cart stands in the forecourt of the Bird Cage Inn. A story in local folklore as to how this inn became so called, is as follows; outside on market days stood a wooden cage for the detention of local rogues when apprehended. At large at this time, was a notorious local thief known as 'the Magpie', but he was caught and detained in the cage, the cry spread around the town, 'The bird is in the cage'. Thereafter the inn became known as the Bird Cage. The Domesday Book records its name only as 'The Cage'.

15. The north side of Cornmarket about 1880, showing Lester's Saddlers with the man standing outside wearing his saddlers apron. This building has been demolished and a shop with flats above it erected, as can be seen in another photograph in this book. The house next door has become a shop, but otherwise still looks the same. This is Middle Row of which, in Edward the first's reign it was recorded that eighteen shops were erected in the market of Thame to the harm of the Royal Dignity, which encroachment was first made in the time of Hugh Trotman, Bishop of Lincoln (1221). The complaint was made as these buildings encroached on the highway 'to the hurt of all passing that way'.

16. This view of Cornmarket showing the Bird Cage Inn was taken about 1920. The cellars of the building were used to house Napoleonic prisoners of war in the years following 1805, and contain an early English arch as would normally be found in a church, the origin of which is unknown. It was these prisoners who founded the local Society of Masons. At one time, timber-framed buildings were considered to be a sign of poverty, consequently these were plastered over to hide the beams. This plaster has been removed from the Bird Cage, thus exposing the beams, so that today we see the half-timbered building looking nearly the same as when it was built.

17. The last building in Cornmarket, next to number 1 High Street, about 1911. The latter became R.A. Styles, then Huntleys bakers and café. The shop to the left was 'Dickey' Bird, the barber. Now it is an opticians. It was later demolished, and together with number 1 High Street, formerly the Fighting Cocks Inn, has become an electrical shop and a supermarket. Behind the Fighting Cocks could be found the Eaton brothers, who were wheelwrights and wagon builders, they would build anything from a wheelbarrow to a large wagon. In 1838 a slaughterhouse and cottage were to be found at the rear of the Fighting Cocks yard, possibly at the Southern Road end.

18. Although the caption reads 'High Street', this is Cornmarket, with the Spread Eagle to the left. This is an early eighteenth century building, having been erected in front of the Crown Inn as a town mansion house in the time of Charles II. Loader and Son, next door, were corn merchants, and were ideally situated, as this street is where corn was traded. The farmers and dealers in corn, would clip trays onto studs let into the wall beneath the ground-floor windows of the Spread Eagle, in which corn samples were displayed. Slater's Chemist is still a chemist shop under a different name, and has continually been a chemist for about 180 years.

THE SPREAD EAGLE HOTEL, THAME

19. The Spread Eagle Hotel in the 1920's, probably at the time when it was owned by John Fothergill, famous for his book 'Diary of an Innkeeper'. He was an eccentric man, refusing to have local people as customers, instead attracting the 'younger set' from London and Oxford. He kept a black eagle in a cage in the hotel foyer, and used to entertain his customers by feeding it with live mice. The bird was one day found dead, possibly due to the actions of drunken guests. In this photograph the trays with the corn samples can be seen on the wall beneath the windows to the rear of the motor cycle. The only change to be seen today, is that the inn sign is no longer projecting from the wall, but is suspended on a post set into the pavement.

Thame.   Butter Market.

20. Buttermarket in the 1880's. Freeman, Hardy and Willis have crossed the road, and now occupy the shop formerly S. and E. Seymour. The inn signs for the Oxford Arms and Saracens Head can be seen here. The town was once notorious for the number of licensed houses it contained. In 1906 there were thirty-five, this number having decreased to thirty in 1915, but even then there was one to each ninety-five of the population. Many have been renamed over the years, the Black Horse being formerly the Mitre, the Fox was the Angel and the Nag's Head was the King's Head. The latter being renamed after the defeat of the Royalists during the Civil War.

21. A street that looks very much the same today. It was formerly called Friday Street, its name being changed after a petition from its inhabitants in 1874. This was probably because of the stigma connected with the word 'Friday', as this day of the week was the one on which handouts to the poor were made. Hence the saying 'as poor as a Friday (or church) mouse'. The large building at the bottom of the street was a wool warehouse, as wool stapling was at one time an important part of the town trade, sometimes the wool leaving the town by special trains. This trade is still carried on in the town today. The house to the left of the photograph, outside of which baskets may be seen, and the one beyond, were demolished to make way for the Grand Cinema, which opened there in 1922. It is now a large toyshop.

22. The rear view of Thame Mill about 1900, then Sydney Pearce's Mill. The water mill was situated on the Aylesbury side of the town and ground corn to provide flour etc. It was built over a mill stream fed from the Cuttle Brook (which marks the Bucks/Oxon border) about half a mile away and drained into the river Thame near the church. This became Thame Mill Laundry in 1931, the wheel being dismantled in the late 1930's, and the building destroyed in a disastrous fire in 1963. A modern building stands in its place, and the mill stream being filled in during the construction of the town bypass.

Victoria Nursing Home, Thame.

23. The Victoria Cottage Hospital, opened in 1897, is pictured here around that time, and was built at the sole expense of Samuel Lacey. The site was bought in East Street for seventy-eight pounds and seventy-five pence, and the hospital built and equipped for seven hundred pounds. Funds were raised, mostly by parades and fetes, to add to it. In 1907 an operating theatre was equipped, in 1922 a three-ward wing was built, as were two maternity wards by 1926, and a further wing for out-patients in the 1960's. It is still in limited use today for convalescence and minor casualties, and fund-raising for further extensions is still under way.

24. Thame Show in 1908, held on the town recreation ground. My introduction records some of the history of this event, it moved to this site in 1897, on Conduit Hill, where it was held for sixty-one years. By the 1920's it included show-jumping, driving nags, cattle, sheep, pigs, poultry and fruit, vegetables etc. In 1922 trade stands were introduced, and a steward for motor traffic appointed. In the 1930-1933 period H.R.H. the Prince of Wales regularly exhibited his alsatian, called Claus of Seale. The show-jumping events here, are an important part of the annual show-jumping calendar, and every year well known riders can be seen taking part in the events.

25. Pictured outside the Vicarage in Long Crendon Road, one of the entries for the pageant held in the Prebendal gardens on 19th July 1923. Around this period processions and galas were very much a feature of the town, some being held annually. A great deal of effort was put into the costumes and scenery, on this occasion, a large replica of the original Elizabethan market hall was built, together with a backdrop depicting the Bird Cage Inn and other buildings in Cornmarket. A carnival was again started as an annual event, in Silver Jubilee year, 1977, and is held on the first Saturday in July after a week of activities. The carnival consists of a procession of colourfully decorated floats, with bands, and culminates with a fete held on the recreation ground.

26. The demolition of the brick-kiln in Park Street. The clay for the making of the bricks here was dug from along the Thame Park Road. This was one of two brick works around the town, the other being sited on Christmas Hill (now Grammar School Hill) alongside Rycote Lane. This kiln was situated at what is now the entrance to Victoria Mead, and part of the low-roofed buildings, the drying kilns, remains today, one end having been demolished and a bungalow built there. The inn sign just visible behind the horse and cart, was probably that of the Red Lion Alehouse, now no longer a public house.

Park Street, Thame.

27. Park Street, looking eastwards from opposite the War Memorial about 1905. This was formerly Brick-kiln Lane, as a kiln was situated at its furthest end, it is the road leading to Chinnor, and most of the buildings are Victorian, although a scattering of older properties can be found along it. The first building to the left, which is in the High Street, is where Rycotewood College was founded with a Mrs. Harley as matron. Later photographs show unsightly telephone poles along this road, and indeed throughout the town. Telephones were installed in 1909, the electricity supply started in 1926. Fortunately all these services are now routed underground.

Park Street, Thame.

28. Park Street looking towards the town, with John Hampden School being the building on the left. This is a junior school, and was founded as the Royal British School in 1836. It was one of the earliest free schools and at the time of its foundation was described as consisting of one long room, with a platform at one end, one small classroom, no cloakroom and the playground mostly ankle-deep in mud. Although extensive buildings have been added in recent years, the frontage is the same today, except for the disappearance of the railings as seen here, these were removed to be melted down to assist the war effort.

29. Chinnor Road carries on from Park Street and along its length was the start of the town's growth during the Victorian period. Consequently most of its property is typically Victorian in design. The side of the road, seen here, is still the same today, it is on the opposite side where modern buildings have been erected. As can so often be seen in pictures of this period, a curious group of children had gathered, anxious to be included in the photograph. The poor state of the road surface can be noticed here, although even that would be better than it was before the houses were built. During the period of 1880 to 1890 a total of sixty houses were built along this road.

CHINNOR ROAD, THAME.

30. Looking towards the town centre, from where Chinnor Road rises to cross the railway by means of a bridge. Behind from where the photograph was taken, stands Essex House, a three-storied building, built to be the railway hotel, as it was thought that the station would be built here. However, it was sited about half a mile nearer the town and the hotel was destined to become a private residence. The right hand side of the road, as seen here, is unaltered development having taken place in the field to the left.

31. Queens Road, about 1910, showing what was then the post office at its junction with Chinnor Road. The town was by now expanding away from those roads leading into and passing through it, these having been specially made for the purpose of building along them. It is rather longer today, than seen here, the opposite side has been built on, also it gives access to the tennis and bowls clubs. It was the former Towersy Road and was built in the area of Thame known as Pickencroft.

32. The Four Horseshoes, which was the 'railway hotel' in Park Street, still looks very much the same today. Its location is opposite the police station, not far from the site of the railway station, and to its left would have stood the brick-kiln. It is interesting to note the advertisements aimed at different types of travellers whether on horseback, by horse-drawn vehicle, on two wheels, or by rail. People would need an over-night stay in the town if they had travelled any distance to visit the market or the fairs, as travel around the turn of the century was slow and uncomfortable. The impact of the motor car, which speeded up these outings, removing the need for such accommodation, was yet to come.

Chinnor Road, Thame.

33. Chinnor Road, at its junction with Thame Park Road. The building to the right is the police station, this having been built in 1857, this is probably the oldest police station in the country. Thame Park is situated about a mile out of the town along the road to the right, this is the Tetsworth Road, and originally ended at the Lodge to Thame Park, known as the Thame Lodge. In December 1863 a locomotive that had been used in the construction of the railway line from Thame to Oxford was being removed on a wagon pulled by twenty-two horses, and opposite the Falcon Inn, that is just out of the right of the picture, it sank into the road, and took many hours to remove. This road is now used by heavy vehicles, as the British Petroleum depot and the Industrial Estate are situated along it, and it is used by traffic bound for London by the M40.

34. East Street about 1880 along which the Cottage Hospital is situated. It is the building beyond the hedge in the centre of the photograph. This road was newly built at about the time this picture was taken, as it was originally a rough road leading to Princes Risborough. The public house between East Street and Park Street is the Cross Keys, and like all the other buildings seen here, is of Victorian origin. The area was mostly occupied by the labouring classes of this period. The town gasworks were situated in the area behind the row of houses to the left of the road.

THAME CHURCH

35. The Parish Church of Saint Mary's looking across Court Close with the vicarage on the right, in about 1895. Building of this splendid church was started about 1240 by Bishop Grosseteste, possibly on the foundations of an earlier church. Due to alterations and extensions, building of it continued until Henry VIII's reign. In pre-reformation times, the church interior was very grand, the plaster work was painted with colourful designs depicting scriptural stories (of which only a small portion remains today) with stained glass windows, ten altars and rich vestments. All that remains today are the early sixteenth century rude screen and the carved oak Jacobean communion table. During the Civil War it was used as a stable, prison, hospital and a barracks. It was restored during the seventeenth and eighteenth centuries.

36. Here we see Lord William's Grammar School, with the Alms House on the right. The school was founded by an endowment in Lord William's will, and building commenced in 1569. It was opened on 29th November 1570 and school hours were from six to eleven in the morning and one to five in the afternoon. Boys had to supply their own candles, pay sixpence per quarter to the undermaster and tuppence for the cleaning of the school and purchase of rods. In its heyday, the school produced such splendid men as John Hampden and John Holt, the latter becoming England's Lord Chief Justice in the early eighteenth century. The school was moved to its present day site, off the Oxford Road in 1879.

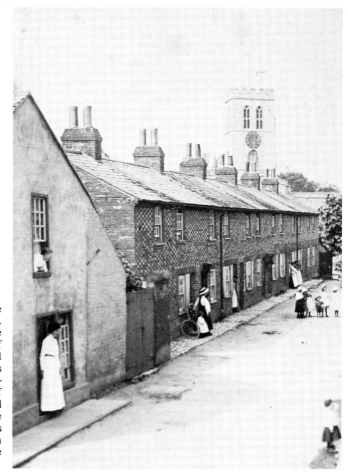

37. Church Road about 1890, along which the Tythe barn is situated, immediately before the church gates. The Alms House is sited along this road opposite the houses. This was established by an endowment of Lord Williams' will, and is a delightful half-timbered building of sixteenth century construction. It was provided for the needy of the town, and accommodated five poor men and women, the cost of housing and clothing them, coming from the annual income of seven pounds four shillings and nine pence from the rents of certain areas of land. The rules governing the occupants were very strict, apart from stipulating the type of clothing they wore, they were forbidden to take in lodgers or to get drunk.

PREBENDAL·LODGE·THAME·OXON.

38. The Prebendal Lodge at about 1890. This is much changed today, as a gatehouse was built across the drive in 1923. This is an attractive stone-built building, in the style of the original lodge. The Prebendal house has been rebuilt by successive owners, some having used the stones from the original buildings. All having been designed to blend in with each other. It is now a private residence which borders on the river Thame facing the Crendon meadows. It was used as a farm for many years, after it passed from Church ownership.

39. The Prebendal chapel and rectory are all that remain of the Prebendal in its original form. The Prebendal was originally founded by a small group of monks whose duties were to collect the tythes (or taxes) due to the church. A list of the prebendaries appointed to Thame has been preserved, and it starts in 1234 and continues until the end of the sixteenth century. The buildings, which were originally of stone, formed a quadrangle with the chapel on the south side and the hall on the east side. In 1661 it was noted that these were in ruins. The chapel was restored in 1912, and became the first Roman Catholic church in the town, before Saint Joseph's Church was built.

40. Situated at the end of Park Street furthest from the town, Newman's Stores was built on the site of a former rifle range. It was here that the local rifle club held their shooting practice. When the shop was first built the floor had not been levelled, and customers walked up a slope from the door to the counter. It occupies an area ajoining the brick-kiln site, the old drying sheds serving as out-buildings behind it. From 1931 until 1973 the business was run as Hunt and Reading's, today, mostly unchanged, it is a pet food shop.

Cattle Market, Thame

41. This view of the cattle market, held in the Upper High Street, was taken about 1900, and shows the late Victorian frontage of the Swan Hotel. This building is of Elizabethan origin, as can be seen inside, the front having been rebuilt after the original one collapsed into the street. The market was a very prosperous one, being held in the Upper High Street, while the market stalls for the sale of vegetables and other goods, were in Cornmarket. The cattle market was moved to a new site, off North Street, in 1951. Today this area is a car park, and the site of the Tuesday market, which is no longer held in Cornmarket.

Cattle Market, Thame

42. Looking towards the town centre, this view of the cattle market in the Upper High Street in about 1900, shows in the centre, the auctioneer's office. This was erected as a chapel by the successors of a group of Presbyterians and Anabaptists. The minister, Matthew Lesson, also ran a school, at which the radical John Wilkes attended as a pupil. The Methodists took over the chapel at the turn of the nineteenth century, moving from it when the new chapel was built in the Upper High Street in 1853. This building is now used as a photographers studio. Both the Methodists and Congregationalists now hold their services in the United Reform Church, formerly the Congregational chapel.

CATTLE MARKET. THAME.

43. The cattle market about 1900, shows how the cattle were tethered to metal posts, erected at the edge of the pavement. In the latter part of the nineteenth, and early twentieth centuries, the market had its difficulties, nearly being closed permanently. It was closed for almost one year when in 1865 rindpest reached Thame, resulting in the deaths of fifteen cattle, and a further eight having to be slaughtered. This disease closed it again from March to June in 1877, as did foot and mouth disease in 1883, and wine fever for seven months in 1894. After threats by the Board of Agriculture to abolish it unless it was improved by paving, the market was cobbled by Sir Francis Bertie in 1904.

44. One of the earliest market scenes to be photographed, dates about 1880. As well as showing the lady's dress of the period, the busy scene emphasises the market's importance at that time. The origins of the town's market date from 1215, the charter being confirmed in 1227, by Henry III. It was declared that no two markets should be held within six and a half miles of each other, consequently most people travelled to the market only during the hours of daylight, to avoid the risks of night travel. For instance, fifteen butchers riding to Thame in 1692 to purchase cattle, were stopped by a gang of marauders, robbed of all their money and compelled to drink the King's health in brandy.

45. Mellett's saddlers was situated in the Upper High Street, the premises now being occupied by a soft-furnishing shop. A fine display of their wares are on show, being mostly heavy horse harness and 'tack', as being in the centre of an agricultural area, there was a heavy demand for this. Shire horses were used for all farming purposes, whether ploughing or pulling carts, as machines had not come into general farm use at the time of this photograph being taken (around 1910). The first steam plough was used in the area in 1857. With this method, two engines were used, one pulled the plough across the field by means of a cable, both moved forward, then it was pulled across in the opposite direction. In the 1830's labourers had destroyed threshing machines at Long Crendon, but as in industry, mechanisation came, particularly with the introduction of the petrol engine.

CORONATION, 1911
THAME, OXON.

46. As elsewhere in the country, Thame celebrated the coronation of King George V in 1911. The siting of the bonfire in the middle of the Upper High Street, was not very wise, but it is rather fortunate that no fire damage was done to surrounding properties. This was a popular area for such fires, at one time youths stole a wagon from Eaton's the wheelwrights, setting fire to it. In the 1850's, 5th November was celebrated with a bonfire here around which the locals let off fireworks, and as snow had fallen, they bombarded a troop of cavalry who were passing through, with squibs and snowballs.

Upper High Street, Thame

47. This view, taken about 1907, shows the great width of the Upper High Street in the market area. To the right can be seen the newly-laid cobbles for the cattle market, and, looking like a fence, the posts for the tethering of the cattle. To the left is White Hound Pond, now filled in, and the site of the Pearce Memorial Gardens, which adjoin the War Memorial. Excepting pavements having been built, and trees planted, this view appears very much the same today. It was in 1906 that Nelson Street was built, making an opening, by demolishing two buildings, in the Upper High Street, thus starting the growth of the town.

48. Thame fire engines, seen outside the old fire engine house. These were horse-drawn vehicles, the pumps worked by hand, and the probable occasion for taking this photograph was the opening of this engine house in 1878. The first fire engine was purchased in 1818, but was most unreliable, a replacement being bought in 1848. In the year 1878, the fire fighting equipment was so poor, that Aylesbury fire brigade (travelling eleven miles) were called to put out a fire in Lashlake. As a result, a new engine was purchased as well as the engine house built.

49. The postal delivery horse and cart are seen here outside the post office at 91 High Street. The post office was in this building from 1885 until 1903, being first situated in Buttermarket, then moving to Cornmarket and finally to its present site at 101 High Street in 1903. A notable postwoman in the early 1800's was Fanny Biggerstaff. She used to carry the post, on foot, to villages in the area, often walking twenty to thirty miles each day, usually carrying the letters in a basket or 'kerchief'. The villagers provided her with gifts of food and drinks – a generosity she relied upon. On one occasion, a letter was stolen from her by a pet monkey whilst she was gossiping.

50. The windmill was situated across the old railway line from what is now the football ground. This is the field in which cricket is being played in this photograph. Today only the house with the double pitch roof remains, this building having once been the Isolation Hospital. The windmill met its end in 1875, due to its all wood construction, when one windy night some youths broke into it and let off the brake. This allowed the windmill to 'run away' in the high wind, causing it to overheat and catch fire. The other windmill in Thame was on Barley Hill, the other two mills being water mills.

51. This picture shows Lashlake Road, now a private road, which runs alongside the church and joins with the Crendon Road. To the right, in the vicarage grounds, can be seen the old Church Rooms, in which Sunday School and Church events were held. This building was demolished after the Church Hall in Nelson Street was built in 1913, which was opened by The Reverend Doctor Spooner, known for his errors in speech which were subsequently called 'spoonerisms'. Lashlake Road was the former Oxford to Aylesbury Road, this having been diverted by Bishop Lexington through the town, to increase the market revenues.

52. This photograph shows the train leaving Thame for Oxford. The view was taken from the Windmill Road level crossing, before 1870, and shows the original Brunel 7 feet broad gauge construction of the track. The building of the railway was commenced in September 1859, and opened in 1862 with Thame as the terminal, the station being built with its roof spanning both tracks. The extension to Oxford was opened in 1864, the track being relaid to standard (4 feet 8½ inches) gauge in 1870. The railway brought benefits to the town, enabling milk and other agricultural produce to be carried fresh to London. Coal became cheaper, and people came to Thame Show and markets from a wider area. It was finally closed in 1963, the line to Oxford being lifted, now it serves only the petrol terminal near the town.

53. Pictured during the 1890's, this shows the north side of the Upper High Street in the market area. Nelson Street, the first development in this part of the town, was built in 1906. The entrance to it was made by demolishing the two buildings shown immediately behind the children. It was built upon the site of Holliers Orchard, and connected with Derrick Street (now Southern Road). White Hound Pond was situated just before the group of trees at the end of the houses. The water in this became so stagnant that horses refused to drink from it, and in January 1859 a lady wandered into it, having to be rescued. The roof and frontage of the former Congregational Church can also be seen.

54. To commemorate the Silver Jubilee of Queen Victoria in 1887, the Town Hall was built, using local brick manufactured at the brickworks on Christmas Hill near Rycote Lane. It replaced the earlier market hall, the site having been purchased from the Earl of Abingdon, for the sum of one hundred pounds. The old hall was pulled down and sold in 68 lots for around fifty-five pounds. The clock is now in Towersey church tower. The town hall cost £2 601.00 to build and still fulfills a useful service to the town today looking the same as seen here, except that the railings have been removed.

55. There are in fact three bridges to be seen in this picture. The first two carry the road over small ponds, known locally as the 'Pills'. The furthest away in the picture and nearest to the town, crosses the river Thame, which here marks the Oxfordshire and Buckinghamshire county boundaries. This road is now closed, as it is cut by the town by-pass at about one hundred yards behind where this photograph was taken. The earlier bridges were washed away by floods on 14th November 1894, cutting the road to Long Crendon. These were subsequently rebuilt, there having previously been arguments as to who was responsible for their repairs. In 1829 it was said that Baroness Wenman, who then owned the Prebendal, was accountable for their upkeep. They were however taken over by the Highway Boards, when these were established, in 1862.

56. Until considerable clearance and dredging work was carried out by the river authorities, serious flooding around Thame was common. Most of the roads into town, except for the Risborough Road, were liable to become impassable. This scene, looking from Thame towards Oxford, shows the floods caused in 1910 when the Cuttle Brook flooded at Ford bridge. Of particular interest is the style of the ladies' fashions, also close examination of the photograph shows that a car is being pulled through the floods by a horse. This is by the trees to the right of the picture.

ONE BELL LANE, THAME OXON.

57. This view shows One Bell Lane, which was so named after the inn once situated just before the entrance to it. The inn lost its licence in 1916 and became the Memorial Club until recently. The building behind the figure was long ago demolished to widen the entrance to what is now known as Bell Lane. The thatched cottages to the left of the road were demolished and the local bus garage was built there. Regular bus services began in April 1922, when the City of Oxford District Motor Bus Services began a service to Thame, taking one hour from Oxford with three services per day on three days every week and two on Sunday.

58. The Spread Eagle was originally a clockmaker's residence and was later rebuilt as a hotel. This photograph from the late 1800's shows the coach possibly destined for Aylesbury. The sign above the arch reading 'B.W. Liddington Job Master', advises that the proprietor hired out horses and carriages. The road to Oxford was along Rycote Lane, the one to London along what is now the bridleway to Tetsworth, where travellers would join the coach at the Swan Hotel. Travel by coach was uncomfortable and also expensive, costing threepence per mile if you sat outside of the coach and fivepence per mile to travel inside, at a speed of about four miles per hour. The coaching inns were spaced about twelve miles apart, this distance being considered the furthest that the horses could pull a coach before needing to be changed for fresh ones.

59. A delightful photograph of a group of children, taken in the Chinnor Road during the late nineteenth century. There are three charming baby carriages to be seen here, as well as showing the style of children's clothing of the period. Although by this time, the quality of housing was greatly improved, living conditions were still primitive by todays standards. Very few homes had a bathroom, which was why public baths were needed, such as those formerly in Buttermarket, also the toilets were outside at the rear of the house. Heating was by a coal or wood fire. The kitchen with its fire in the 'range' heating the room and doing the cooking, became the room most lived in during the winter months. The doors and windows would have been draped with heavy curtains to keep out the draughts.

60. This view shows Priestend from the bottom of High Street, looking towards Oxford in about 1895. Opposite the figure is the entrance to Rycotewood Agricultural College, formerly the town work-house. This was built during 1836-37, to accommodate 350 men and women, and served thirty-five parishes in the area. The accommodation it provided was spartan and as there were only dormitories to live in, the men, women and children were kept separate. The poor did not wear a uniform although clothing was provided, and able-bodied men and women had to carry out menial tasks, such as unpicking hemp, but they were well provided for both with food and medical attention.

61. Thame Literary Institute was started in a small house in the market place. Its aims were 'The furtherance of general knowledge, the checking of intemperance and immorality, and to rouse the mind to the pursuit of higher and worthier objects'. It was in existence in 1857, and contained an extensive library, to which frequent additions were made by the generosity of local people. It also held frequent group discussions (although religion and politics were forbidden subjects for debate) some of these being very lively and on strange and obscure subjects. It outgrew these premises, moving to 91 High Street in 1910, into the former post office building and it was the forerunner of the public libraries we have today. It can be seen here in the three-storied building on the right of the photograph.

62. The Oxfordshire Yeomanry frequently held parades in the town, and camped nearby. In this photograph of the troops marching along East Street at its junction with Kingsey Road by the Star and Garter public house, taken in 1907, one of the mounted officers is Winston Churchill, seen here with Major B.W. Liddington, the landlord of the Spread Eagle Hotel, and Captain C.F. Howland, both prominent figures in Thame at that time. Troops were often billetted in the town when on their way to manoeuvres. The object of this was to attract local recruits, as they were the local professional soldiers. Their presence in or around the town was sure to bring out the youths of Thame in great numbers.

63. In 1911, the Great Western Railway was instructed to move a great number of troops, by rail, from Thame railway station. This is depicted here. Many lessons were learned from this, thus enabling troop movements for the First World War to be carried out smoothly. The soldiers marched right through the town, from the Oxford end, and the town people turned out in force to cheer them on their way. This was an important occasion, as well as a complicated one, the railway having to arrange for the transportation of horses, supply wagons and so forth, as well as the men themselves.

64. These men were volunteers lining up in Thame Upper High Street to sign up for the First World War. Of those who came forward, 587 men were enlisted. Those unsuitable for active service were drafted into the Volunteers for guard duties. The old Boys Grammar School was turned into a hospital, the old Almshouse adjoining, being used as a gymnasium and the town hall as an orderly room and offices. The town's people did all they could to help the war effort and the first women farm workers were seen in the area. The town also received refugees from Belgium, for the duration of the war. Children from London's East end were brought here to spend two weeks holiday in the comparitive peace of the country.

65. This picture shows the procession from King Edward VII's memorial service in Thame. This service was very well attended, as he was a well-loved King despite his short reign of only nine years. The service was conducted at Saint Mary's Church, after which those who had been present were led back into the town by a military band together with representatives of the armed forces. The fashions of the period can be clearly seen here, ladies skirts still sweeping the ground. It was not until after the First World War that these became shorter, and clothes generally more casual, with the difference between the rich and the poor showing far less in the clothing they wore.

THE HOUSE IN WHICH JOHN HAMPDEN DIED.
JUNE 24TH. 1643. THAME.

66. John Hampden who was a student of Lord Williams' Grammar School, is a figure well known to students of history. His refusal to pay 'ship-money', led to his imprisonment in 1627, being released the following year. These events led indirectly to the King making a declaration of War on parliament on the 22nd August 1642, which meant that England was now in the throes of a Civil War. The Parliamentarians established their headquarters in Thame on the tenth of June 1643 and on the seventeenth of June, Prince Rupert led his Royalist troops out of Oxford, halting at a field at Chalgrove, these were attacked by Cavalier forces with John Hampden leading a troop on horseback. During the battle he was wounded in the shoulder, but managed to ride his horse back to Thame, to the Greyhound Inn in the High Street, where he had rooms. In spite of medical attention he died here on the 24th June 1643. After the licence of the inn lapsed, it became shops, and another Greyhound Inn was established at the top of Moorend Lane, this now being three cottages. This view shows the building as it was in 1915.

LORD WILLIAM'S GRAMMAR SCHOOL
THAME, OXON. H.H.

67. This is Lord William's Grammar School on its present site, as seen about 1890. It was opened here on 1st May 1879. Today it is almost surrounded by modern buildings, as it is now a comprehensive school catering for a wide area around the town. Also in its grounds stands a new Sports and Arts Centre, the most recent addition to the amenities it offers. When it opened, it was exclusively a boys Grammar School, only those of high academic standard attending there. It is situated upon a low hill to the west of the town, and set amid extensive playing fields.

NOTLEY MILL, BUCKS
H.M.N°

68. Although Notley Abbey is situated in Buckinghamshire, it is little more than on the outskirts of Thame. The mill stood on the river Thame and was used to grind corn produced in the area. All that remains of this are the two arches over the river and mill stream, this having been demolished some time after it was photographed in 1904. The abbey was founded as a home for Augustinian canons about 1135, one of their obligations being to pray for the souls of Henry II and his Queen. Of the original buildings, none now remain, a large mansion house having been built in its place, some of the old stones being used in its construction. For some years this was the home of Vivien Leigh and Laurence Olivier, the famous film-stars.

St Joseph's Church Thame

69. Saint Joseph's Catholic Church was built in Brook Lane, during 1922, meetings having previously been held in the Prebendal Chapel. The building, originally of brick with rough cast exterior and asbestos tiled roof, has now been much improved. The building seen beyond was the National School, built on the site of the old Hog Fair in 1838, to which an infant school was added in 1842. The buildings were demolished in 1967 and a small housing development now occupies the site. The Hog Fair was an area of land, owned by the Earl of Abingdon, which was used for such 'entertainments' as fighting, between dogs and cockerels also boxing and bull baiting.

70. Shown here is a Temperance parade in Thame High Street about 1910. These parades were a regular feature in the town, being usually held on Easter Mondays. These societies came into being due to social changes, at that time resulting partly from the working people earning better wages and the brewers being able to produce beer more cheaply. It was felt that this led to social problems, as money was being spent freely on drink, supposedly leaving the family in debt, possibly facing eviction from their homes and the threat of violence induced by alcohol. The aim of this society was to persuade people to abstain from intoxicating drink, which was termed as 'the curse of man'.

71. The Almshouses are seen here at the time that they were being used as tea-rooms during the 1920's. These were no longer being used by the poor, who were now housed in more suitable property by the council. They ceased to be used as Almshouses during the 1920's, the pensioners receiving £33.6s 8d per year in lieu of all rights. During the First World War, when the Grammar School was used as a hospital, the Almshouses were used as a gymnasium by the patients, one of the floors in one part of the building being removed for this purpose.

Thame War Memorial

72. Thame War Memorial was built on land donated by the Lord of the Manor, Lord Bertie, adjoining the White Hound Pond. It was unveiled by the Right Honorable Lloyd George M.P.O.M. Prime Minister of England, on 30th July 1921. A guard of honour was formed by the Queen's own Oxfordshire Hussars, and the Oxfordshire and Buckinghamshire Light Infantry. Out of a population of 2,957, Thame sent 587 officers and non-commissioned officers and men to serve in the First World War. Of these, 87 were killed and 200 wounded, a considerable proportion of the men of the town thus having fought in this war. The ceremony was attended by some 6,000 people, including the chairman and members of the Thame Urban District Council. During his speech Lloyd George said: 'I was here fourteen years ago at a review of the Oxfordshire Yeomanry. I believe the present Lord Chancellor was one of the officers present.' This was the occasion when Winston Churchill was an officer with the troops at camp on Barley Hill.

THE MARKET, THAME OXON.

73. This shows an unusual view of Thame market, seen here from the south side of the Upper High Street near to the start of Cornmarket. The row of cottages between Putman's and the Oxford Arms is no longer there, as those to the right have become part of the Putman building (Barclays Bank until recently), the others are an extension of the Oxford Arms, which now has a mock Tudor front. The telegraph poles have long since been removed, so improving the appearance of the town, and the street market which can be seen in Cornmarket, is now held in the area to the right of the picture.

74. Seen here is the west front of Thame Park in 1895. This is a Palladian front built in 1745, all that remains of the abbey being the south front. Contrary to information given on many maps, there are no ruins remaining, nor is the house accessible to the public. The abbey was founded as a Cistercian monastery in 1130 on Otmoor and transferred to Thame about 1140. Its first abbot was Everadus. The monks rebuilt both their own and the abbot's lodgings in the sixteenth century, the tower being of twelfth century construction. There also remains the church, which has been restored, this and the house passing into private hands at the Reformation. One of the owners, Lady Wenman, had a fear of being buried alive, and decreed that she should be buried in the crypt of the church in a glass-topped coffin, fitted with air ventilation. This is still there today, her body having been interred in the family vault. During the Second World War, the house and grounds were used to train undercover agents who operated in German-occupied France.

75. North Street seen here at the turn of the century. The boy on the pavement to the right, carrying a basket with a convex base, is almost certainly a chimney sweep boy. He would climb up inside the chimney to the top, and sweep the soot into the basket with a brush, the rounded base of the basket being so designed to enable it to slide freely down the chimney. There is recorded locally a tragedy involving one of these boys. It seems he got wedged inside the chimney, unable to move up or down. His master however, thinking he had fallen asleep, lit a fire in the hearth which caused the boy's death. The children in the centre of the picture look as if they might have been purchasing buns from the baker.

76. This shows one of the first steam rollers seen in the area when the roads around the town were being improved from the muddy, rutted tracks they had become. In 1894, a steam roller was hired to roll the granite, which was being used at that time, to provide a suitable surface. Even the town roads were very poor, Buttermarket not being laid with cobblestones until 1908. Tarmac was not used in the town until the High Street was tarred in 1911, the area from the Town Hall to Bell Lane not being so treated until 1913. The steam engine seen here was owned by the Oxfordshire Steam Ploughing Company, such a firm being well suited to turning to road building, as they were experienced in handling steam engines.